Mighty Fun Activities for Practising Times Tables, Book 1

2, 5 and 10 Times Tables

Hannah Allum
Hannah Smart

Brilliant
PUBLICATIONS

We hope you and your pupils enjoy the activities in this book. Brilliant Publications publishes many other books for use in primary schools. To find out more details on any of the titles listed below, please log onto our website: www.brilliantpublications.co.uk.

Published by Brilliant Publications Limited
Unit 10
Sparrow Hall Farm
Edlesborough
Dunstable
Bedfordshire
LU6 2ES, UK

Website: www.brilliantpublications.co.uk
Tel: 01525 222292

The name Brilliant Publications and the logo are registered trademarks.

Written by Hannah Allum and Hannah Smart
Illustrated by Gaynor Berry
Cover by Brilliant Publications Limited and Gaynor Berry

© Text Hannah Allum and Hannah Smart 2016
© Design Brilliant Publications 2016

Printed ISBN: 978-1-78317-267-2
ebook ISBN: 978-1-78317-271-9

First printed and published in the UK in 2016.

Contents

Introduction...4
A quick introduction to the sheets...........5
Meet the mighty sporty superheroes! 6

2x table
Superhero wrist watch – 2x table 7
Supersonic Sinitta's mask 8
Stolen – Sinitta's superhero outfit!.............9
Great hoops of fire!................................10
Race for superpowers 11
Trainer trail 12
Supersonic goodies! 13
Dragon breath!.......................................14
Sprint challenge.....................................15
Changing room problems 16
Draw the answer.....................................17
Solve the code..18

5 x table
Superhero wrist watch – 5x table 19
Mighty Justice John's mask....................20
Muddled score cards 21
Rescue the javelin tips!..........................22
Crack the code! 23
Top score! 24
Javelin pathways 25
Pop the force field!................................26
Javelin search!.......................................27
Danger! Poisonous bubbles! 28
Save the colours!...................................29
Shoot for the clouds...............................30

10x table
Superhero wrist watch – 10x table 31
Mighty Jet Pack Jim's mask 32
Planet adventure 33
Super boosts! 34
Find the missing jet packs 35
Help Jim get his superpowers! 36
Jump to the planets 37
Kit delivery...38
Flight paths 39
Journey to Plant Long Jump!...................40
Coded capers! 41
Mighty word problems 42

Mixed
Missing numbers 43
Number trails 44
Burst the stars 45
Mighty dive! 46
Pop the air bubbles................................47
Race to the sweet..................................48
Colour the dragons.................................49
Rocket code...50
Superhero boosts 51
Mighty high jumping!..............................52

Answers to code sheets 53

Introduction

The *Mighty Fun Activities for Practising Times Tables* series uses superheroes to motivate children to practise all of the skills needed to solve multiplication, division and word based times table problems. Superheroes appeal to even the most reluctant of learners and instil a positive and competitive attitude towards learning. The aim is for children to become excited and motivated enough to want to learn and practise their times tables.

The mighty superheroes are based upon the sporty characters in our highly popular whole-school reward-based scheme, *The Mighty Multiples Times Table Challenge*. The sheets in this book can be used in conjunction with the series or independently.

There are three books in the *Mighty Fun Activities for Practising Times Tables* series:
Book 1:   2, 5 and 10 times tables
Book 2:   3, 4, 6 and 8 times tables
Book 3:   7, 9, 11 and 12 times tables

The books contain reproducible sheets and are designed to be used as flexible teaching aids which teachers can dip in and out of in any order to support the learning of any times table. They work equally well as stand alone 5 to 20 minute lesson reinforcements or as regular times table learning.

We recognise that all children learn in different ways and that they need to have opportunities to apply their knowledge and skills. For each times table there is a mixture of practical activities to develop their understanding and written activities to consolidate their knowledge.

There is also an exciting wrist watch and mask for each times table for children to make and wear. These can be used as an introduction to each character or to consolidate learning. Children will become mightily good at their times tables by using their mighty powers! Looking at their watch or mask is a fun and exciting way to memorise the times tables.

The mixed times table sheets at the back of the book allow children to apply the skills gained in learning individual tables, working out for themselves which multiple facts and methods they need to use.

The answers to the code sheets are given on page 53.

A quick introduction to the sheets

Approximate time needed to complete the main activity on the sheet. The time can be altered to suit individuals or groups of children who require more or less time. Children will enjoy the challenge of beating **Dennis the Demon Digit Demolisher** and will feel a sense of pride and achievement if they can successfully beat the super villain.

Times table covered by sheet is clearly stated.

Read the instructions aloud if necessary so that pupils are clear what they have to do.

Children can self-assess how well they feel they have done by colouring in the circles:
1 circle = I need a bit of help please.
2 circles = I'm getting there.
3 circles = I've got it!

Danger! Poisonous bubbles!

`15:00` `5x`

`How did you do?`

Dennis the Demon Digit Demolisher has sent poisonous gloop bubbles into the air above the javelin field. Help **Mighty Justice John** pop them with his javelin before they get a chance to settle. Solve the questions in the bubbles to help him.

8 x 5 ___
1 x 5 ___
35 ÷ 5 ___
5 x 5 ___
1 x 5 ___

4 x 5 ___
10 ÷ 5 ___
10 x 5 ___
12 x 5 ___
45 ÷ 5 ___

7 x 5 ___

25 ÷ 5 ___
40 ÷ 5 ___
3 x 5 ___
15 ÷ 5 ___
55 ÷ 5 ___

2 x 5 ___
9 x 5 ___

6 x 5 ___
30 ÷ 5 ___

20 ÷ 5 ___
50 ÷ 5 ___

5 ÷ 5 ___

Home Challenge
Write multiples of 5 on pieces of card. Place them face down. Turn over as many as you can in 2 minutes, shouting out how many groups of 5 make the number on the card.

Mighty Challenge
Can you think of word problems to go with answers 40 and 25?

Mighty Fun Activities for Practising Times Tables, Book 1
28

©Hannah Allum, Hannah Smart and Brilliant Publications
This page may be photocopied for use by the purchasing institution only.

The Home Challenges provide practical and physical learning activities that can be assigned as homework. They have been designed to encourage parents to join in as their children develop their times table knowledge at home in an active way.

The Mighty Challenges allow children to self-extend and apply the skills which have been targeted during the activity even further.

Meet the mighty sporty superheroes!

In this book you will meet three mighty sporty superheroes (and some of their friends):

Mighty Supersonic Sinitta
The 2x table champion

Mighty Justice John
The 5x Table Champion

Mighty Jet Pack Jim
The 10x Table Champion!

These mighty sporty superheroes are taking part in the ***Trans-galaxy Superhero Games***! Their mission is to practise their times tables along the way, demonstrating mighty skills in multiplying, dividing, and solving word problems!

There is, however, one problem! A super villain named ***Dennis the Demon Digit Demolisher*** and his pet, ***Lorraine the Loathsome Dragon***, have an evil plan to make a world without numbers!

Can you help the mighty superheroes work their way through each event and stop super villain ***Dennis the Demon Digit Demolisher*** from sabotaging the events?

You will have to be mighty clever, mighty quick and mighty resourceful!

Good luck!

Superhero wrist watch - 2x table

Can you make your own superhero wrist watch for *Mighty Supersonic Sinitta*'s 2x table? Complete the questions, then cut out and wear the wrist watch.

1 x 2 = ☐
2 x ☐ = 4
☐ x 2 = 6
4 x 2 = ☐
5 x ☐ = 10
☐ x 2 = 12
7 x 2 = ☐
☐ x 2 = 16
2 x ☐ = 18
10 x 2 = ☐
11 x 2 = ☐
☐ x 2 = ☐

Home Challenge

Put a number card 1–12 on each stair in your house! When you walk upstairs, jump on the numbers and multiply them by 2.

Mighty Challenge

Can you continue to multiply numbers by 2 up to 20?

Supersonic Sinitta's mask

Can you finish *Mighty Supersonic Sinitta*'s superhero mask by filling in the answers? Decorate the mask, but take care not to colour over the questions as you will lose your superpowers!

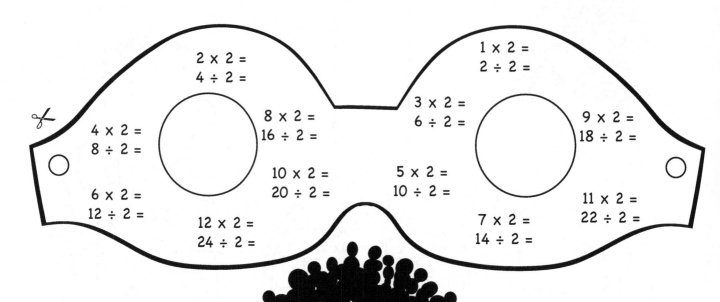

$2 \times 2 =$
$4 \div 2 =$

$1 \times 2 =$
$2 \div 2 =$

$8 \times 2 =$
$16 \div 2 =$

$3 \times 2 =$
$6 \div 2 =$

$4 \times 2 =$
$8 \div 2 =$

$9 \times 2 =$
$18 \div 2 =$

$10 \times 2 =$
$20 \div 2 =$

$5 \times 2 =$
$10 \div 2 =$

$6 \times 2 =$
$12 \div 2 =$

$11 \times 2 =$
$22 \div 2 =$

$12 \times 2 =$
$24 \div 2 =$

$7 \times 2 =$
$14 \div 2 =$

Home Challenge

Can you make a 2x cloak to match? Whiz around your house looking for numbers to multiply by 2.

Mighty Challenge

Can you write any more questions on your mask? Can you multiply some 3 digit numbers by 2?

Stolen - Sinitta's superhero outfit!

Dennis the Demon Digit Demolisher has stolen *Mighty Supersonic Sinitta*'s superhero outfit. She has a race in 10 minutes. Help her by answering the questions to shoot her outfit back to her.

Home Challenge

As you sort the washing out, count all the items, then times that number by 2. How many does that make?

Mighty Challenge

If you times all of the items on the washing line by 2, how many would you have?

Great hoops of fire!

10:00   2x

How did you do?

Dennis the Demon Digit Demolisher **has set all the hula hoops on fire! Help**
Mighty Supersonic Sinitta **to put them out. Help her to jump through the hoops by**
answering the questions.

5 x 2 =

7 x 2 =

2 x 4 =

11 x 2 =

6 x 2 =

3 x 2 =

2 x 10 =

9 x 2 =

2 x 12 =

Home Challenge

How long can you hula hoop for,
whilst saying your 2x tables?

Mighty Challenge

Can you draw lines to join the hoops
from the lowest to the highest answer?

Race for superpowers

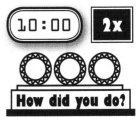

Mighty Supersonic Sinitta is racing *Dennis the Demon Digit Demolisher* to save the planet. Every question she answers on the hurdles makes her 2x faster. Help her to become mighty speedy!

START

FINISH

$5 \times 2 =$

$10 \times 2 =$

$2 \times 12 =$

$4 \times 2 =$

$3 \times 2 =$

$11 \times 2 =$

$7 \times 2 =$

$9 \times 2 =$

$2 \times 8 =$

Home Challenge

Go for a walk with your family. Count how many people you see on your travels. Now times that number by 2.

Mighty Challenge

What is $13 \times 2 = ?$, $14 \times 2 = ?$, $15 \times 2 = ?$ How high can you go?

Trainer trail

Help *Mighty Supersonic Sinitta* by drawing lines to join her trainers, counting in 2s. You will need to be mighty quick, before *Dennis the Demon Digit Demolisher* hides any!

Home Challenge

How quickly can you put your trainers on? Count in 2s as you do it and write your time here:

_____.

Mighty Challenge

Can you continue the pattern by adding 3 more trainers? What numbers will they have on them?

Supersonic goodies!

10:00   2x

How did you do?

Can you help *Mighty Supersonic Sinitta* to share her superhero goodies between herself and her best friend *Mighty Hypersonic Heather*?

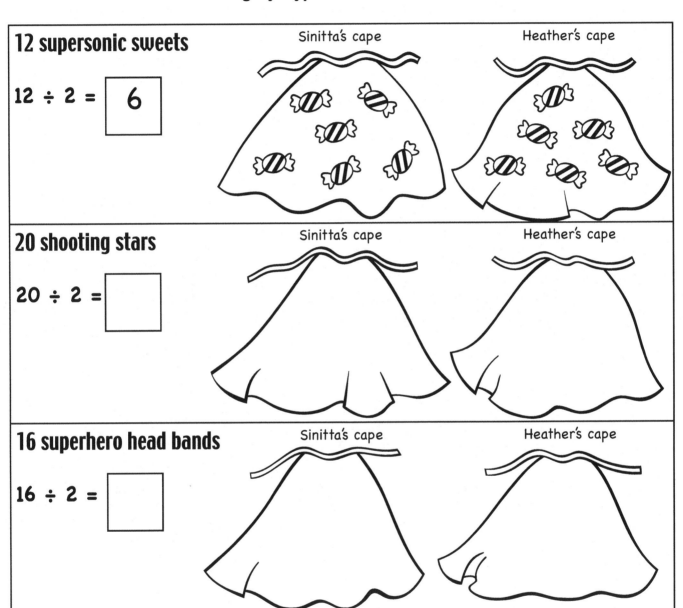

12 supersonic sweets

$12 \div 2 = \boxed{6}$

Sinitta's cape   Heather's cape

20 shooting stars

$20 \div 2 = \boxed{}$

Sinitta's cape   Heather's cape

16 superhero head bands

$16 \div 2 = \boxed{}$

Sinitta's cape   Heather's cape

Home Challenge

Can you share all the fruit in your fruit bowl between you and one other person? How many pieces of fruit did you have each?

Mighty Challenge

Sinitta sorts her fruit bowl fairly between herself and her friend Heather. If she gave herself 12 pieces of fruit, how many pieces of fruit did they start with?

Mighty Fun Activities for Practising Times Tables, Book 1

Dragon breath!

Lorraine the Loathsome Dragon is breathing out drops of energy juice! She wants to make sure that *Dennis the Demon Digit Demolisher* gets it all! Beat him to it by answering the questions on the drops to make them evaporate!

$14 \div 2 =$

$8 \div 2 =$

$20 \div 2 =$

$12 \div 2 =$

$10 \div 2 =$

$16 \div 2 =$

$4 \div 2 =$

$6 \div 2 =$

$18 \div 2 =$

$2 \div 2 =$

Home Challenge

Blow some bubbles in the bath. As you pop each one, say a multiple from the 2x table.

Mighty Challenge

Imagine you have 24 cups of water. Can you share them between 2 people. How many did each person have?

Sprint challenge

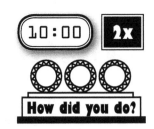

10:00 2x

How did you do?

Mighty Supersonic Sinitta is competing in a sprint challenge against the other superheroes. Help her to solve the answers and pop all the balloons, as each balloon contains superpowers!

7 × 2

8 ÷ 2

14 ÷ 2

10 × 2

12 × 2

24 ÷ 2

20 ÷ 2

5 × 2

6 × 2

Home Challenge

Ask a friend or family member to write some 2x questions on balloons. Answer them. Pop the balloon if correct. How many did you pop?

Mighty Challenge

Can you add 5 more balloons with 2x or ÷ 2 questions on them?

Changing room problems

Each of *Mighty Supersonic Sinitta*'s capes has a 2x table question or a ÷ 2 question on it. Each one needs to hang on a peg with the correct answer on it. The peg numbers have fallen off. Can you cut them out and stick them on?

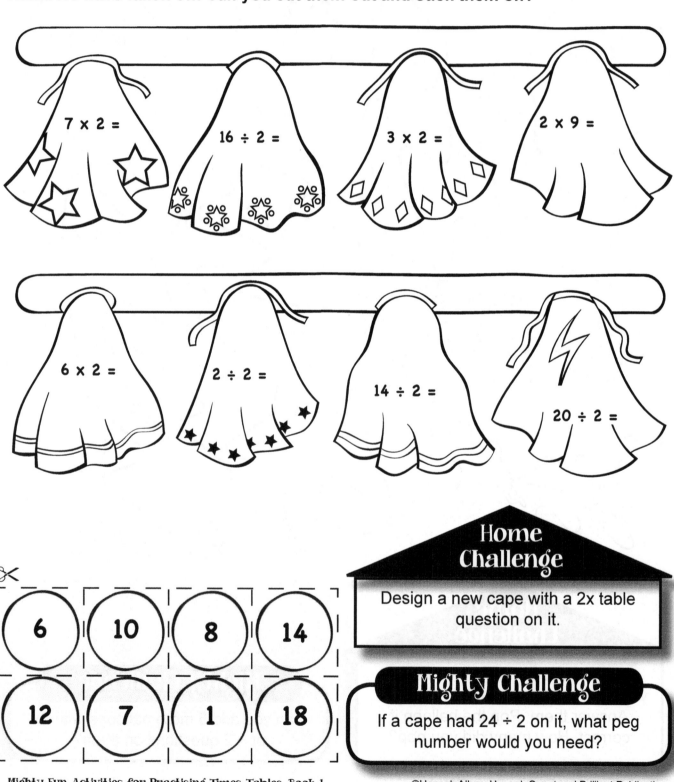

7 × 2 =

16 ÷ 2 =

3 × 2 =

2 × 9 =

6 × 2 =

2 ÷ 2 =

14 ÷ 2 =

20 ÷ 2 =

| 6 | 10 | 8 | 14 |
| 12 | 7 | 1 | 18 |

Home Challenge

Design a new cape with a 2x table question on it.

Mighty Challenge

If a cape had 24 ÷ 2 on it, what peg number would you need?

Draw the answer

Help *Mighty Supersonic Sinitta* to solve these problems. Draw pictures to help you work out your answers. See if you can beat *Dennis the Demon Digit Demolisher*'s time of 25 minutes.

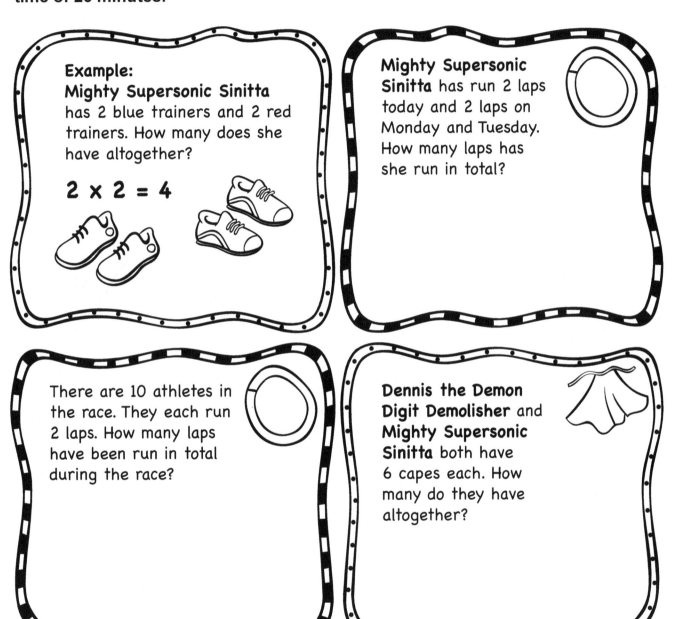

Example:
Mighty Supersonic Sinitta has 2 blue trainers and 2 red trainers. How many does she have altogether?

$2 \times 2 = 4$

Mighty Supersonic Sinitta has run 2 laps today and 2 laps on Monday and Tuesday. How many laps has she run in total?

There are 10 athletes in the race. They each run 2 laps. How many laps have been run in total during the race?

Dennis the Demon Digit Demolisher and **Mighty Supersonic Sinitta** both have 6 capes each. How many do they have altogether?

Home Challenge

Run round the park 2 x 5 times.

Mighty Challenge

If each of the 8 athletes wins 2 stickers for their superhero cape, how many stickers were handed out?

Mighty Fun Activities for Practising Times Tables, Book 1

Solve the code

How did you do?

Answer the questions and find the letter next to the number.

_____ ☐ = 4 × 2

_____ ☐ = 12 ÷ 2

_____ ☐ = 9 × 2

_____ ☐ Sinitta has 8 tickets. She shares them with Mighty Jet Pack Jim. How many do they have each?

_____ ☐ = 10 ÷ 2

_____ ☐ = 2 × 7

_____ ☐ = 24 ÷ 2

_____ ☐ = 1 × 2

_____ ☐ There are 10 superheroes on each of the 2 teams. How many superheroes are in the race?

_____ ☐ = 8 × 2

_____ ☐ = 22 ÷ 2

_____ ☐ Each of the 11 athletes needs 2 hurdles. How many need to be put out?

_____ ☐ = 4 ÷ 2

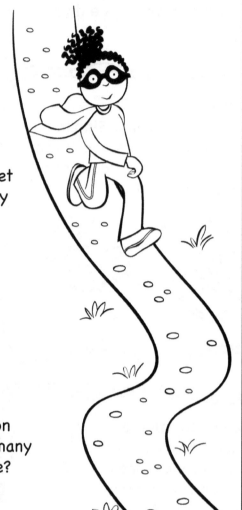

A = 11	
B = 21	
C = 13	
D = 27	
E = 9	
F = 16	
G = 14	
H = 12	
I = 5	
J = 56	
K = 24	
L = 10	
M = 4	
N = 18	
O = 40	
P = 0	
Q = 72	
R = 8	
S = 22	
T = 2	
U = 6	
V = 19	
W = 28	
X = 1	
Y = 20	
Z = 7	

Home Challenge

How many times can you run up and down the stairs, reciting your 2x times tables backwards?

Mighty Challenge

Using the letter values above, try to write questions and answers that would spell your name.

Answer

___ ___ ___   ___ ___ ___ ___ ___
___ ___ ___ ___

Superhero wrist watch - 5x table

Can you make your own superhero wrist watch for *Mighty Justice John*'s 5x table? Complete the questions, then cut out and wear the wrist watch.

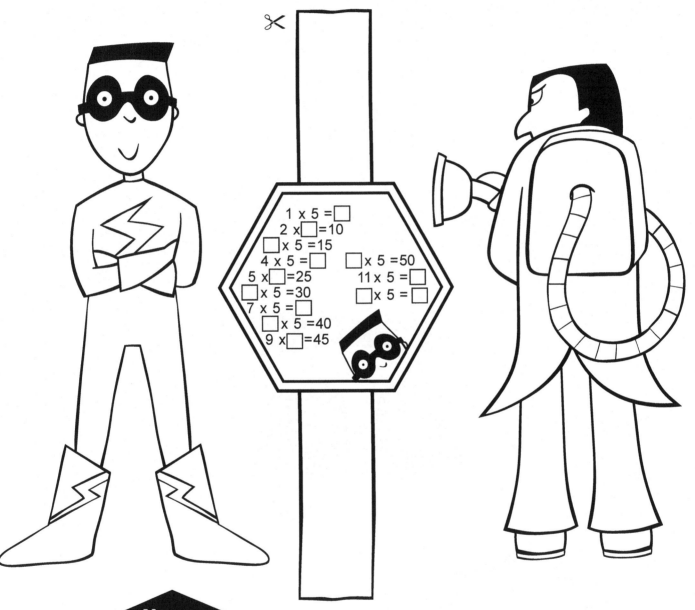

1 x 5 =☐
2 x☐ =10
☐ x 5 =15
4 x 5 =☐   ☐ x 5 =50
5 x☐ =25   11 x 5 =☐
☐ x 5 =30   ☐ x 5 =☐
7 x 5 =☐
☐ x 5 =40
9 x☐ =45

Home Challenge

Wear your watch on a walk with an adult. Look for numbers around you and see if you can multiply them by 5.

Mighty Challenge

Can you write multiples of 5 on your wrist watch band?

Mighty Justice John's mask

15:00 5x

How did you do?

Can you finish *Mighty Justice John*'s superhero mask by filling in the answers?
Decorate the mask, but take care not to colour over the questions as you will lose
your superpowers!

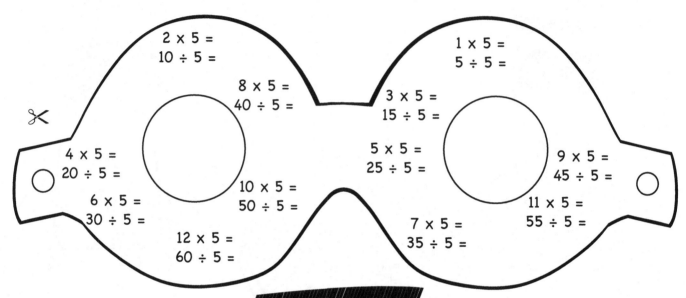

2 x 5 =
10 ÷ 5 =

8 x 5 =
40 ÷ 5 =

4 x 5 =
20 ÷ 5 =

6 x 5 =
30 ÷ 5 =

10 x 5 =
50 ÷ 5 =

12 x 5 =
60 ÷ 5 =

1 x 5 =
5 ÷ 5 =

3 x 5 =
15 ÷ 5 =

5 x 5 =
25 ÷ 5 =

9 x 5 =
45 ÷ 5 =

11 x 5 =
55 ÷ 5 =

7 x 5 =
35 ÷ 5 =

Home Challenge

Can you make masks for all your
family? You have to beat *Dennis the
Demon Digit Demolisher* – so get
the 5x table written down quickly!
Can you beat your family to multiply
numbers in your house by 5?

Mighty Challenge

Are the answers in the 5x table factors
of any other table you know?

Muddled score cards

How did you do?

Dennis the Demon Digit Demolisher has muddled up all of *Mighty Justice John*'s score cards, so no one can understand how many points they have won! Solve the questions and draw lines to the correct answers to help *Mighty Justice John* to find out how much each competitor scored.

2 x 5 = ____

4 x 5 = ____

6 x 5 = ____

12 x 5 = ____

8 x 5 = ____

11 x 5 = ____

1 x 5 = ____

5 x 5 = ____

9 x 5 = ____

3 x 5 = ____

7 x 5 = ____

10 x 5 = ____

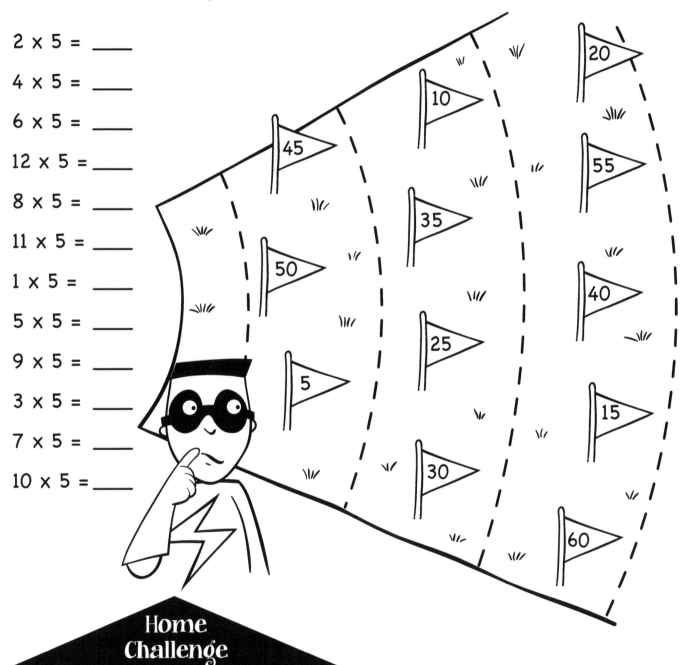

Home Challenge

Blow up some balloons. Write a multiple of 5 on each balloon. Ask an adult to ask you questions. Rush and pop the correct answer

Mighty Challenge

Can you answer these questions?
13 x 5 =   17 x 5 =   18 x 5 =

Rescue the javelin tips!

Mighty Justice John has to check the javelins before the competition, but *Dennis the Demon Digit Demolisher* has got there first. He has taken the tips off the javelins and thrown them in the mud! Can you help *Mighty Justice John*? Solve the questions on the handles and colour in the tips when you find the answers.

12 x 5 =

11 x 5 =

6 x 5 =

9 x 5 =

7 x 5 =

3 x 5 =

1 x 5 =

10 x 5 =

2 x 5 =

5 x 5 =

4 x 5 =

8 x 5 =

15   45   55   30   50   35   25   20   40   60   10   5

Home Challenge

Run round the house looking for *Dennis the Demon Digit Demolisher*. When you think you see him, count to 60 in 5s!

Mighty Challenge

Can you write all the multiples of 5 between 60 and 100?

Crack the code!

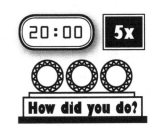

20:00   5x

How did you do?

Dennis the Demon Digit Demolisher is trying to steal all *Mighty Justice John*'s javelins so that he can't compete in the event. Can you help *Mighty Justice John* to find a good pace to hide his javelins by cracking the code?

7 x 5 = ☐ ___

1 x 5 = ☐ ___

10 x 5 = ☐ ___

5 x 5 = ☐ ___

2 x 5 = ☐ ___

8 x 5 = ☐ ___

9 x 5 = ☐ ___

5 x 1 = ☐ ___

4 x 5 = ☐ ___

11 x 5 = ☐ ___

7 x 5 = ☐ ___

5 x 10 = ☐ ___

5 = N
10 = E
15 = G
20 = D
25 = H
30 = R
35 = I
40 = S
45 = A
50 = T
55 = P
60 = O
65 = Y

Answer

_ _   _ _ _

_ _ _ _ _ _ _

Home Challenge

Can you roll a die and then hop along, counting up in 5s, from the number on the die?

Mighty Challenge

Can you think of a better place to hide the javelins? Write your own code.

Mighty Fun Activities for Practising Times Tables, Book 1

Top score!

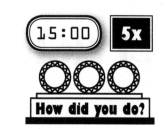

Mighty Justice John wants to beat his top score! He has to throw the javelins 5x as far as the numbers on the posts. But *Dennis the Demon Digit Demolisher* is trying to get to them first! Can you help *Mighty Justice John*? Times the scores on the posts by 5 to discover the new scores.

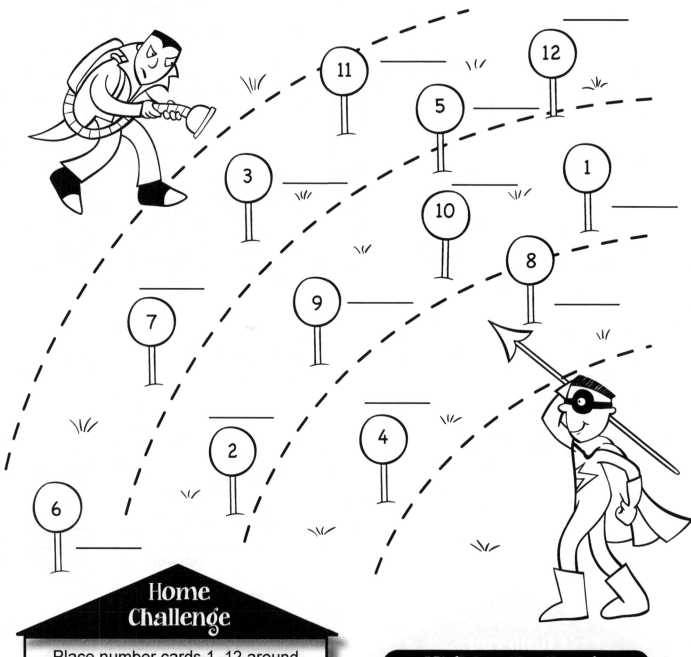

Home Challenge

Place number cards 1–12 around your garden. Throw a cardboard tube javelin at them and multiply the number by 5.

Mighty Challenge

Can you add some more numbered score posts and multiply them by 5?

Javelin pathways

15:00 5x

How did you do?

Dennis the Demon Digit Demolisher has put secret motors inside the javelins. Help *Mighty Justice John* to steer the javelin and keep on the pathways counting in 5s.

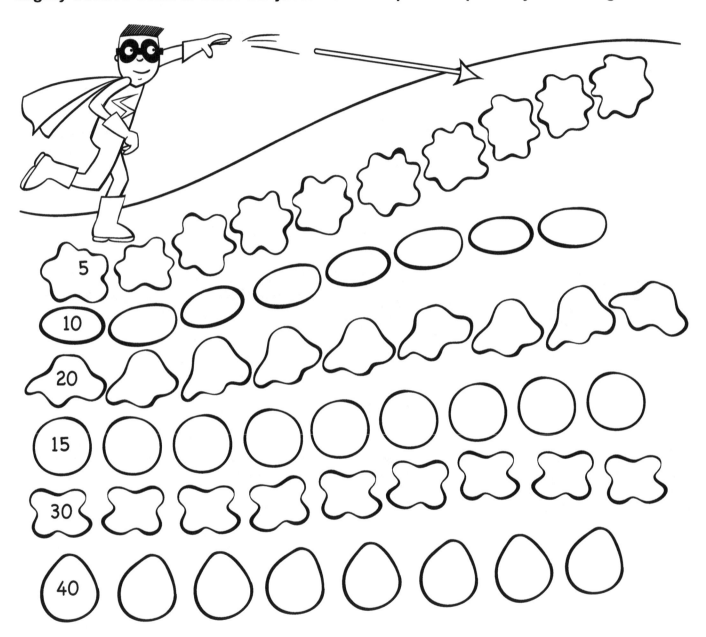

5
10
20
15
30
40

Home Challenge

Look for a number on a door or a sign. As you walk towards the number, try to say your complete 5x table before you reach the number!

Mighty Challenge

Can you draw some more pathways, but start with numbers that are not factors of 5?

Pop the force field!

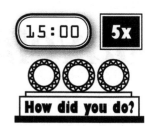

15:00   5x

How did you do?

Dennis the Demon Digit Demolisher has thrown all the javelins up into force fields. Can you help *Mighty Justice John* to answer the questions on the javelins and use them to pop the force fields. Colour in the force fields when you find the answers.

Home Challenge

Blow some bubble mix in the air and pop as many bubbles as you can whilst counting in 5s.

Mighty Challenge

Roll 2 dice add the numbers and divide by 5! Are there any remainders?

Javelin search!

Dennis the Demon Digit Demolisher has hidden all the javelins in a space race! Can you fly into space with *Mighty Justice John* and see if you can hit the stars with your javelins before the super villain catches you? Write your answers on the javelin tips.

$25 \div 5 =$

$60 \div 5 =$

$15 \div 5 =$

$40 \div 5 =$

$50 \div 5 =$

$30 \div 5 =$

$5 \div 5 =$

$10 \div 5 =$

$55 \div 5 =$

$35 \div 5 =$

$20 \div 5 =$

$45 \div 5 =$

Home Challenge

Can you look up at the stars at night and use your finger to point to each one counting in 5s?

Mighty Challenge

Choose 3 of the stars and write word problems to go with them.

Mighty Fun Activities for Practising Times Tables, Book 1

Danger! Poisonous bubbles!

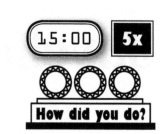

15:00 **5x**

How did you do?

Dennis the Demon Digit Demolisher has sent poisonous gloop bubbles into the air above the javelin field. Help *Mighty Justice John* pop them with his javelin before they get a chance to settle. Solve the questions in the bubbles to help him.

8 x 5 ____

1 x 5 ____

35 ÷ 5 ____

5 x 5 ____

1 x 5 ____

4 x 5 ____

10 ÷ 5 ____

10 x 5 ____

12 x 5 ____

45 ÷ 5 ____

25 ÷ 5 ____

40 ÷ 5 ____

3 x 5 ____

15 ÷ 5 ____

7 x 5 ____

55 ÷ 5 ____

6 x 5 ____

30 ÷ 5 ____

2 x 5 ____

9 x 5 ____

20 ÷ 5 ____

5 ÷ 5 ____

50 ÷ 5 ____

Home Challenge

Write multiples of 5 on pieces of card. Place them face down. Turn over as many as you can in 2 minutes, shouting out how many groups of 5 make the number on the card.

Mighty Challenge

Can you think of word problems to go with answers 40 and 25?

Mighty Fun Activities for Practising Times Tables, Book 1
28

Save the colours!

Dennis the Demon Digit Demolisher has made all the colours disappear from the javelin event competitors' uniforms! Can you help *Mighty Justice John* to save the day? Solve the questions and use the key to put the colours back on their clothes.

5 = green
6 = red
7 = blue
10 = black
15 = orange
20 = yellow
55 = pink
50 = purple

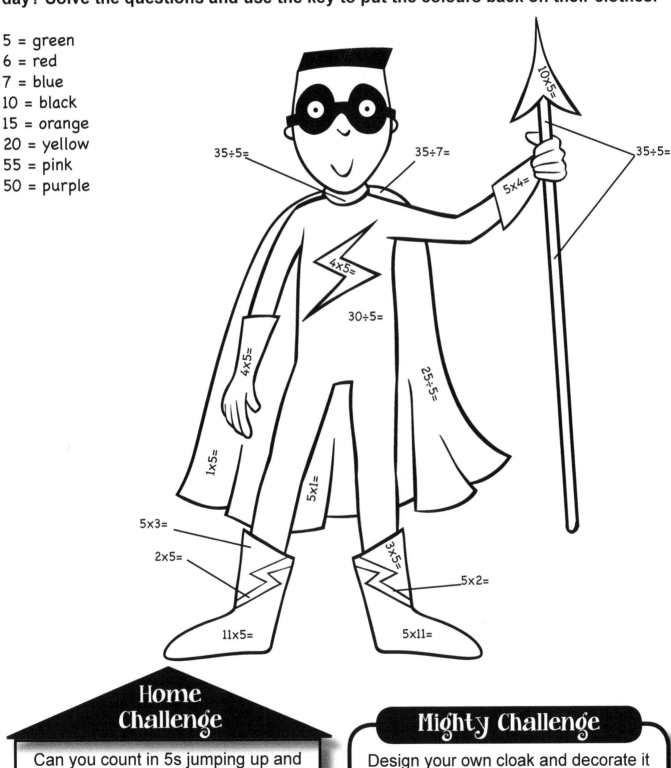

Home Challenge

Can you count in 5s jumping up and down?

Mighty Challenge

Design your own cloak and decorate it with multiples of 5.

Shoot for the clouds

Mighty Justice John is practising his javelin throwing skills. Help him to solve the questions on the clouds and shoot the javelin with the correct answer to each cloud.

Before he started throwing his javelin, **Mighty Justice John** lay down watching the clouds in preparation. He watched for 5 minutes and saw 9 clouds each minute. How many was that in total?

If there were 5 superheroes in each round of the competition and 7 rounds, how many javelins were thrown?

Every year **Mighty Justice John** is given 5 new javelins. He has been a superhero athlete for 11 years. How many javelins does he have now?

Mighty Justice John has entered 4 competitions. In each one he throws 5 javelins. How many does he throw altogether?

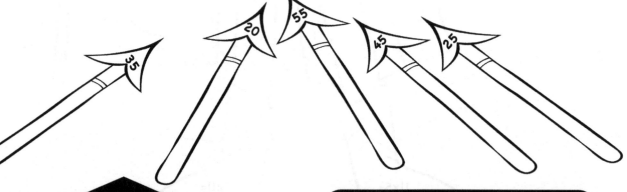

Home Challenge

Use an empty kitchen roll to make a javelin for *Mighty Justice John*. Make sure it's mighty good by writing all the multiples of 5 on it.

Mighty Challenge

Mighty Justice John had to pay £5 to everyone who threw their javelin further than he did. 12 people did this. How much money did he have to pay altogether?

Superhero wrist watch - 10x table

Can you make your own superhero wrist watch for *Mighty Jet Pack Jim*'s 10x table? Complete the questions, then cut out and wear the wrist watch.

1 x 10 = ☐   ☐ x 10 = 100
☐ x 10 = 20   ☐ x ☐ = 110
3 x 10 = ☐   12 x 10 = ☐
☐ x 10 = 40
5 x 10 = ☐
☐ x 10 = 60
7 x ☐ = 70
8 x 10 = ☐
9 x 10 = ☐

Home Challenge

Put 1–12 number cards on the floor. Jump to every number multiplying it by 10!

Mighty Challenge

Can you write the whole 10x table in less than 30 seconds?

Mighty Jet Pack Jim's mask

Can you finish *Mighty Jet Pack Jim*'s superhero mask by filling in the answers? Decorate the mask, but take care not to colour over the questions as you will lose your superpowers!

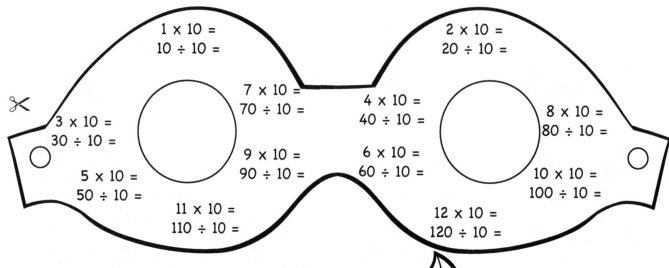

1 x 10 =
10 ÷ 10 =

2 x 10 =
20 ÷ 10 =

7 x 10 =
70 ÷ 10 =

4 x 10 =
40 ÷ 10 =

3 x 10 =
30 ÷ 10 =

8 x 10 =
80 ÷ 10 =

9 x 10 =
90 ÷ 10 =

6 x 10 =
60 ÷ 10 =

5 x 10 =
50 ÷ 10 =

10 x 10 =
100 ÷ 10 =

11 x 10 =
110 ÷ 10 =

12 x 10 =
120 ÷ 10 =

Home Challenge

Wear your mask to the supermarket. Every time you put another item in the trolley, multiply the total number of objects by 10!

Mighty Challenge

Can you multiply all the answers on your mask by 10? Then 10 again?

Planet adventure

Each planet has a question on it. Answer the questions then help *Mighty Jet Pack Jim* jump around the answers in order, joining them up from the lowest number to the highest.

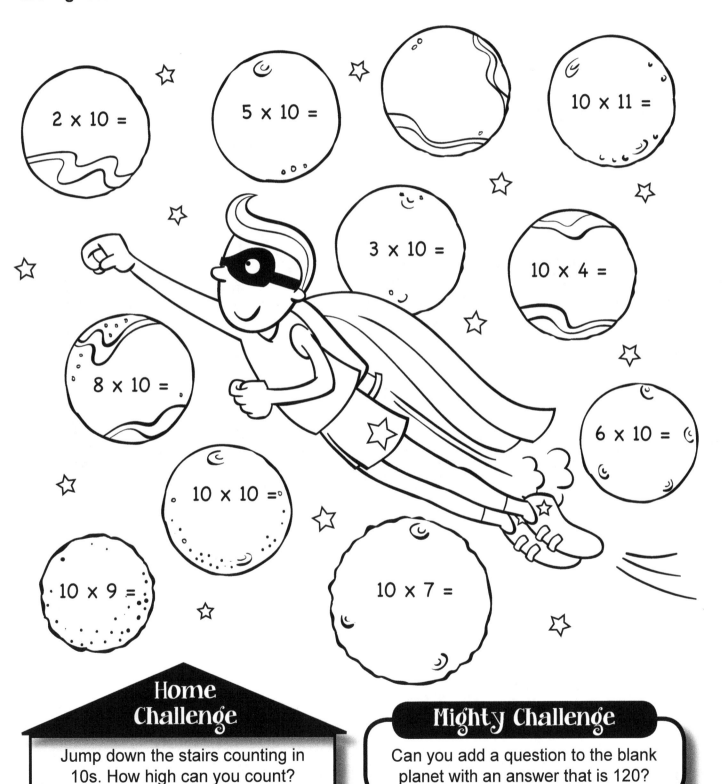

2 × 10 =

5 × 10 =

10 × 11 =

3 × 10 =

10 × 4 =

8 × 10 =

6 × 10 =

10 × 10 =

10 × 9 =

10 × 7 =

Home Challenge

Jump down the stairs counting in 10s. How high can you count?

Mighty Challenge

Can you add a question to the blank planet with an answer that is 120?

Super boosts!

05:00   10x

How did you do?

Mighty Jet Pack Jim can earn extra super boosts by jumping to the stars and solving the problems. If he solves a problem, you can colour it using superhero colours! How many superhero stars can you create in 5 minutes?

5 x 10 =

11 x 10 =

2 x 10 =

9 x 10 =

4 x 10 =

3 x 10 =

7 x 10 =

8 x 10 =

12 x 10 =

1 x 10 =

Home Challenge

Can you jump and try to catch the stars whilst saying your 10 times table?

Mighty Challenge

What is the highest number you can x by 10?

Find the missing jet packs

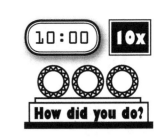
Mighty Jet Pack Jim has mislaid his jet packs! Help him to find all the jet packs that have a multiple of 10 on them. If you find one, colour it in.

Home Challenge

Can you design a new jet pack for *Mighty Jet Pack Jim*, with a number from the 10x table on it?

Mighty Challenge

Can you add some more jet packs that are multiples of 10?

Mighty Fun Activities for Practising Times Tables, Book 1

Help Jim get his superpowers!

15:00 10x

How did you do?

Colour in *Mighty Jet Pack Jim*'s path in 10s, to allow him to gain his superpowers!

Start

68
11
10
5
30
45
20
52
40
50
44
60
99
60
92
70
110
120
45
80
90
100

Finish

Home Challenge

Put some multiples of 10 on cards on the floor. When your friend gives you a 10x question, jump to the right answer.

Mighty Challenge

Can you jump across the room whilst counting in 10s?

Jump to the planets

10:00   10x

How did you do?

Can you help *Mighty Jet Pack Jim* to jump to each of the planets using his superpowers by solving these questions?

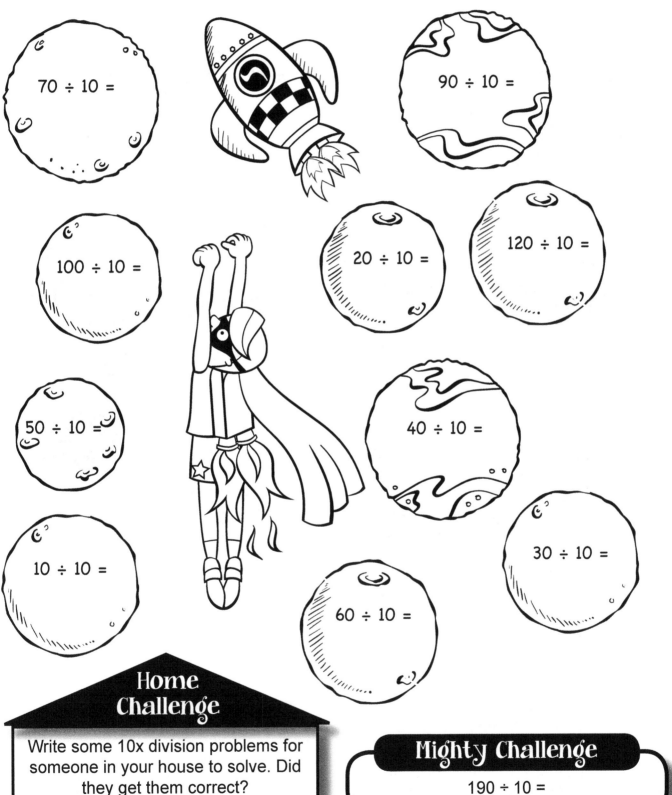

$70 \div 10 =$

$90 \div 10 =$

$100 \div 10 =$

$20 \div 10 =$

$120 \div 10 =$

$50 \div 10 =$

$40 \div 10 =$

$10 \div 10 =$

$30 \div 10 =$

$60 \div 10 =$

Home Challenge

Write some 10x division problems for someone in your house to solve. Did they get them correct?

Mighty Challenge

$190 \div 10 =$

Mighty Fun Activities for Practising Times Tables, Book 1

Kit delivery

Mighty Jet Pack Jim has received a mighty delivery of kit for the next jump. He needs to share the kits between the 10 contestants. Can you help him?

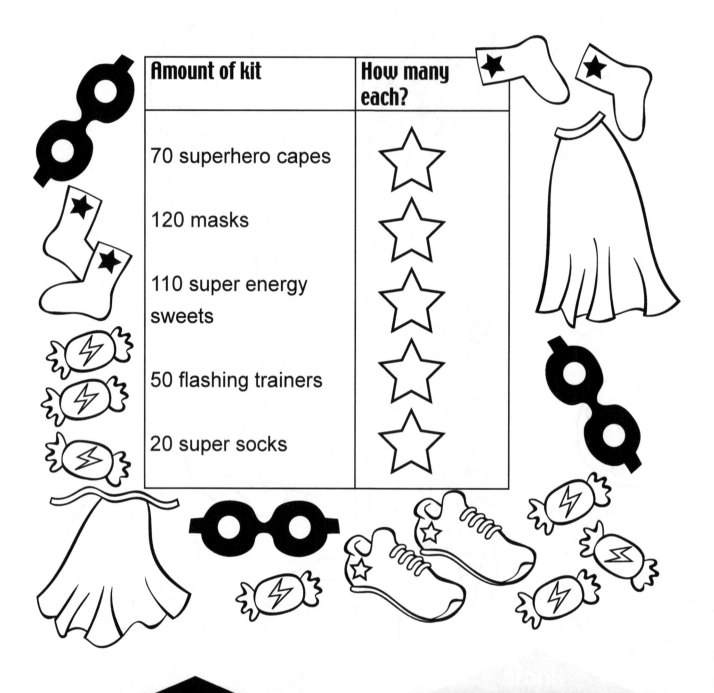

Amount of kit	How many each?
70 superhero capes	☆
120 masks	☆
110 super energy sweets	☆
50 flashing trainers	☆
20 super socks	☆

Home Challenge

Can you find 3 x 10 items of clothing in your house?

Mighty Challenge

If each jump should be 4 metres, how many metres would be covered by 10 jumpers?

Flight paths

Can you help *Mighty Jet Pack Jim* fly along the paths, filling in the missing numbers as you go?

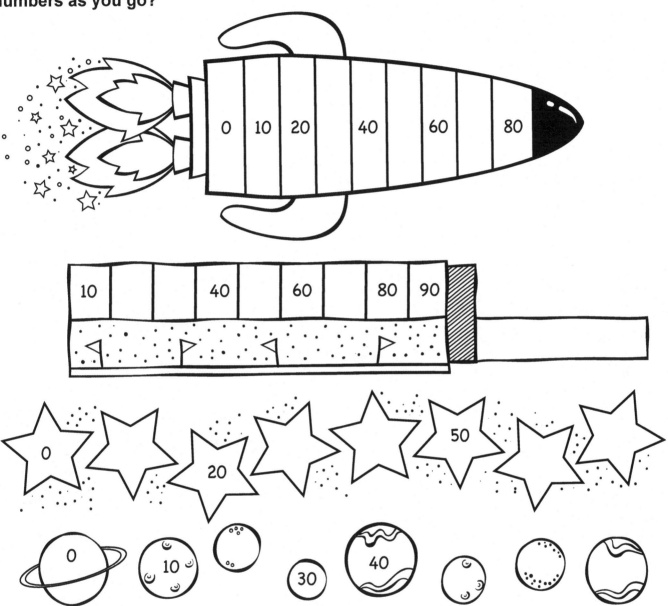

Mighty Challenge

Add some more paths. Can you try some that do not have a zero in the units holder?

Journey to Planet Long Jump!

Mighty Jet Pack Jim needs to jump round the planets and answer the questions to get to Planet Long Jump. See if you can help!

Home Challenge

Dress as a superhero and fly around the room answering 10x and ÷ 10 questions that your family shoot at you.

Mighty Challenge

On his last journey to Planet Long Jump, *Mighty Jet Pack Jim* made 10 stops. He answered the same amount of questions at each stop and answered 60 in total. How many questions did he answer at each stop?

Coded capers!

15:00 10x

How did you do?

To take part in the next superhero mission, *Mighty Jet Pack Jim has* to solve the code on his cape. Help him to do so before the starting gun goes off!

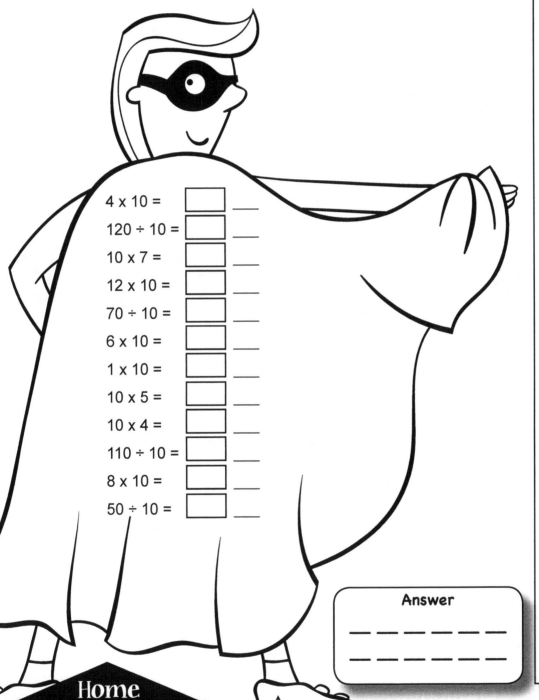

4 x 10 = ☐ ___

120 ÷ 10 = ☐ ___

10 x 7 = ☐ ___

12 x 10 = ☐ ___

70 ÷ 10 = ☐ ___

6 x 10 = ☐ ___

1 x 10 = ☐ ___

10 x 5 = ☐ ___

10 x 4 = ☐ ___

110 ÷ 10 = ☐ ___

8 x 10 = ☐ ___

50 ÷ 10 = ☐ ___

A = 20	
B = 132	
C = 2	
D = 130	
E = 80	
F = 0	
G = 70	
H = 120	
I = 12	
J = 10	
K = 42	
L = 90	
M = 40	
N = 96	
O = 67	
P = 11	
Q = 14	
R = 5	
S = 77	
T = 7	
U = 50	
V = 146	
W = 30	
X = 100	
Y = 60	
Z = 17	

Answer

_ _ _ _ _ _ _

_ _ _ _ _ _ _

Home Challenge

Hop around the room saying your 10x table in a superhero voice.

Mighty Challenge

Can you divide 140 by 10?

Mighty Fun Activities for Practising Times Tables, Book 1

Mighty word problems

Your challenge: find the answers to *Mighty Jet Pack Jim*'s mighty word problems. Write the answers in the little stars.

Mighty Jet Pack Jim jumped 8 times. Each time he drank 10 sips of an energy drink. How many sips did he have altogether?

To warm up, **Mighty Jet Pack Jim** has to do 10 jumps, 10 skips and 10 hops. How many moves is that altogether?

Watching the mighty jump were 10 rows of spectators. Each row had 10 super seats. How many super seats were there?

During one day of the superhero competition **Mighty Jet Pack Jim** enters 10 challenges. For each one he jumps twice. How many jumps did he complete in total?

Home Challenge

Write word problems with the number 10 in them for everyone in your house.

Mighty Challenge

If 120 people came to watch the competition, how many rows of 10 seats would they need to put out?

Missing numbers

Dennis the Demon Digit Demolisher has wiped all the race numbers off the superhero capes. Help write them back on. They must be multiples of their times tables.

Mighty Justice John (5x tables)

Mighty Supersonic Sinitta (2x tables)

Mighty Jet Pack Jim (10x tables)

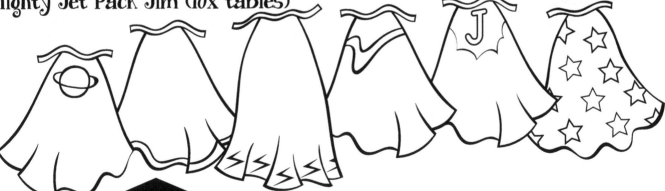

Home Challenge

Design a cape with your favourite times table on it. Add the multiples of your table in bright colours.

Mighty Challenge

Can you add 2 more capes for each superhero?

Mighty Fun Activities for Practising Times Tables, Book 1

Number trails

The superheroes are having a swimming race. To win they have to join the numbers, counting up in their tables.

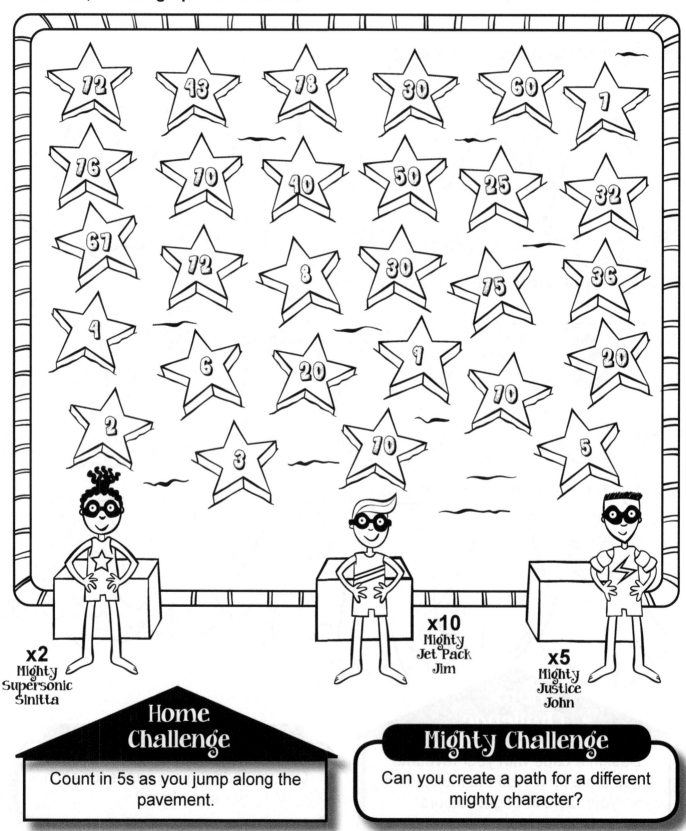

Home Challenge

Count in 5s as you jump along the pavement.

Mighty Challenge

Can you create a path for a different mighty character?

Burst the stars

Each star contains a special superhero power. Answer the questions to burst the stars and release the powers.

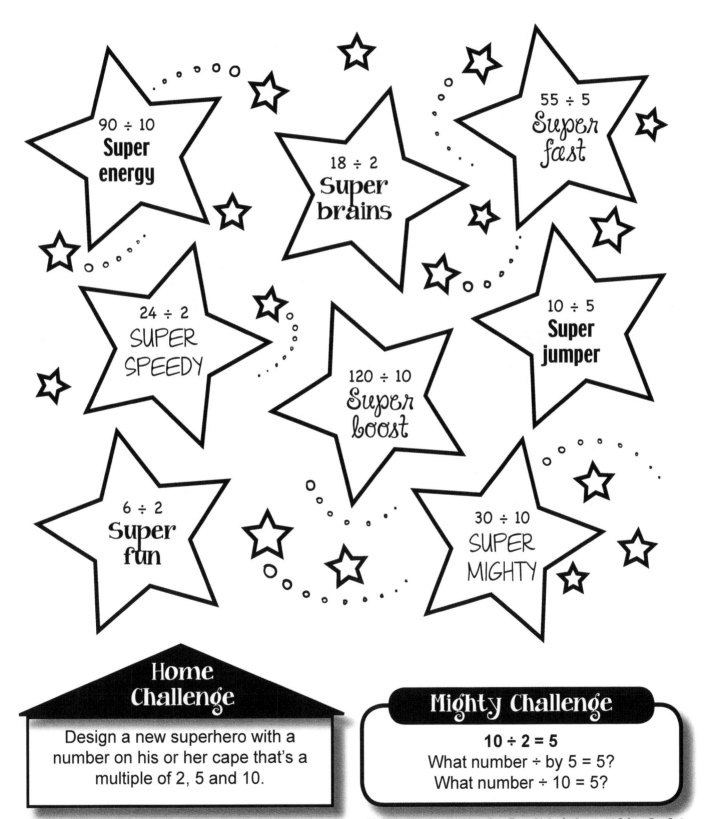

90 ÷ 10 **Super energy**

18 ÷ 2 **Super brains**

55 ÷ 5 *Super fast*

24 ÷ 2 SUPER SPEEDY

120 ÷ 10 *Super boost*

10 ÷ 5 **Super jumper**

6 ÷ 2 **Super fun**

30 ÷ 10 SUPER MIGHTY

Home Challenge

Design a new superhero with a number on his or her cape that's a multiple of 2, 5 and 10.

Mighty Challenge

10 ÷ 2 = 5
What number ÷ by 5 = 5?
What number ÷ 10 = 5?

Mighty Fun Activities for Practising Times Tables, Book 1

Mighty dive!

Dennis the Demon Digit Demolisher has scored 60 points in the diving competition. Now it's *Mighty High Dive Clive*'s turn. Help him to dive into the pool and pick a superhero item and solve the question on it. Each correct answer earns 10 points.

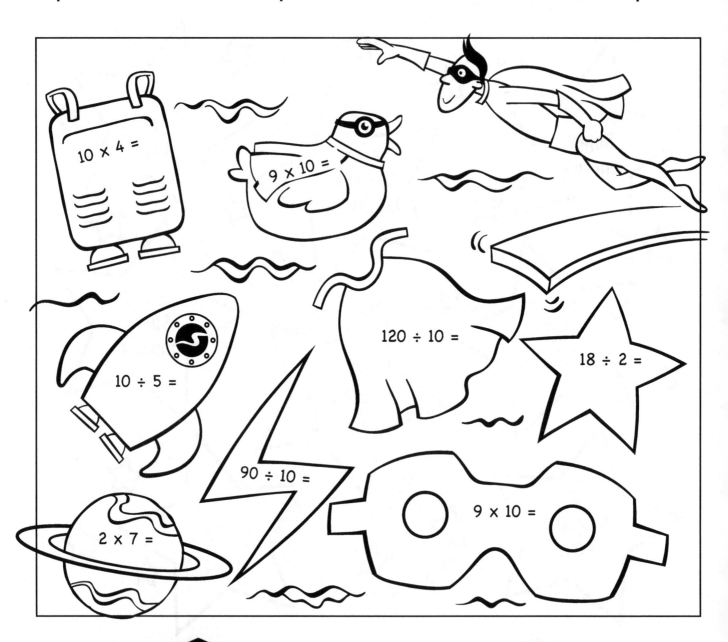

Home Challenge

Whilst brushing your teeth try counting backwards in 2s from 24 in your head.

Mighty Challenge

If I added 6 more items and you scored top marks, how many points would you score in total?

Pop the air bubbles

Dennis the Demon Digit Demolisher is trying to pop all of the air bubbles in the pool. Help *Mighty High Dive Clive* to dive down and solve the questions to create more!

10 ÷ 2

120 ÷ 10

45 ÷ 5

50 ÷ 10

30 ÷ 10

70 ÷ 10

4 ÷ 2

50 ÷ 10

25 ÷ 5

24 ÷ 2

6 ÷ 2

18 ÷ 2

Home Challenge

Blow bubbles in the bath. Pop them whilst counting in 5s.

Mighty Challenge

If *Dennis the Demon Digit Demolisher* popped 2 bubbles a second for 10 seconds, how many would he pop?

Mighty Fun Activities for Practising Times Tables, Book 1

Race to the sweet

The superheroes are racing to win the **Mighty Energy Sweet**. Time yourself answering the questions for each superhero. See which column you answer the quickest – that superhero wins!

8 x 2
2 x 7
9 x 2
2 x 10
12 x 2
5 x 2

12 x 10
8 x 10
4 x 10
10 x 5
10 x 7
2 x 10

5 x 5
9 x 5
2 x 5
7 x 5
5 x 11
10 x 5

Mighty Supersonic Sinitta

Mighty Jet Pack Jim

Mighty Justice John

Home Challenge

Lay in the garden at night. Each time you spot a star, shout out a number from the 10x tables.

Mighty Challenge

Colour in any answers that are part of the 2, 5 and 10 times tables.

Colour the dragons

15:00   Mixed

How did you do?

Lorraine the Loathsome Dragon and her friends have stolen all the multiples of 2, 5 and 10. The superheroes need to blast their footballs at them to get them back. If the multiple belongs to 2, colour the dragon red; if it belongs to 5, colour it yellow; if it belongs to 10 colour it green. If it is a multiple of 2 or more numbers, use a mix. For example, for 10 use all 3 colours!

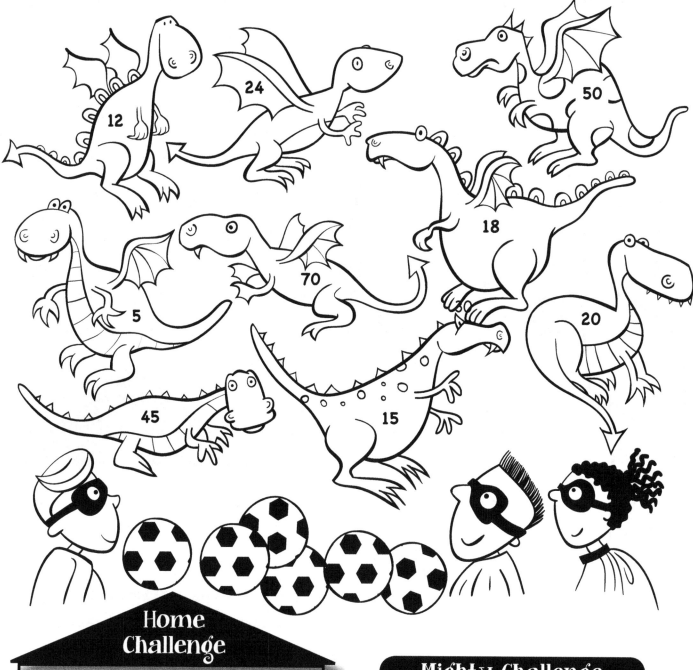

Home Challenge

Kick a football in the air. Before it lands, how many times can you say the 5 times table?

Mighty Challenge

Add an extra dragon for each of the superheroes.

Rocket code

Crack the code to find the winner of this round of the competition.

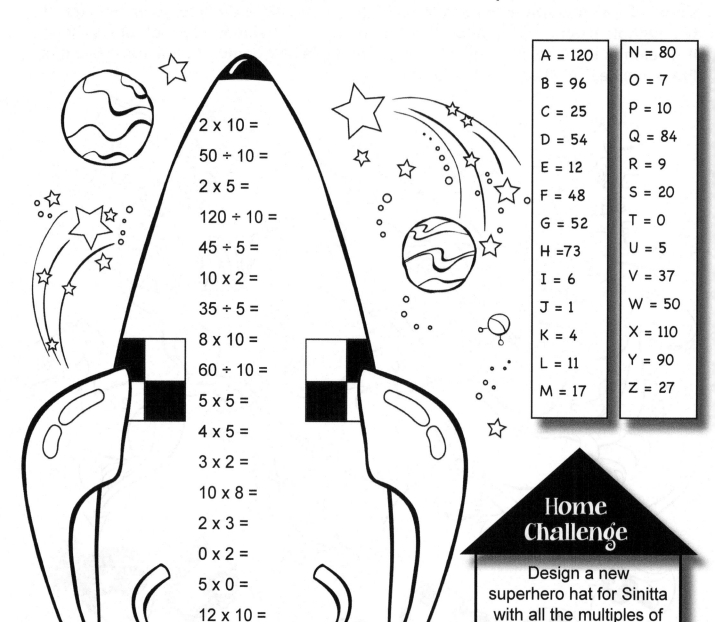

A = 120	N = 80
B = 96	O = 7
C = 25	P = 10
D = 54	Q = 84
E = 12	R = 9
F = 48	S = 20
G = 52	T = 0
H =73	U = 5
I = 6	V = 37
J = 1	W = 50
K = 4	X = 110
L = 11	Y = 90
M = 17	Z = 27

2 x 10 =

50 ÷ 10 =

2 x 5 =

120 ÷ 10 =

45 ÷ 5 =

10 x 2 =

35 ÷ 5 =

8 x 10 =

60 ÷ 10 =

5 x 5 =

4 x 5 =

3 x 2 =

10 x 8 =

2 x 3 =

0 x 2 =

5 x 0 =

12 x 10 =

Home Challenge

Design a new superhero hat for Sinitta with all the multiples of 2 on it.

Mighty Challenge

Select 2 of the questions. Can you use them to write the different questions that can be made. For example:

2 x 5 = 10   10 ÷ 5 = 2

5 x 2 = 10   10 ÷ 2 = 5

Answer

_ _ _ _ _ _ _ _ _ _ _

_ _ _ _ _ _ _ _

Superhero boosts

20:00 Mixed

How did you do?

Help *Mighty High Dive Clive* to reach the stars by answering the questions on the diving boards to reach the top. Each level gives him 5 superhero boosts.

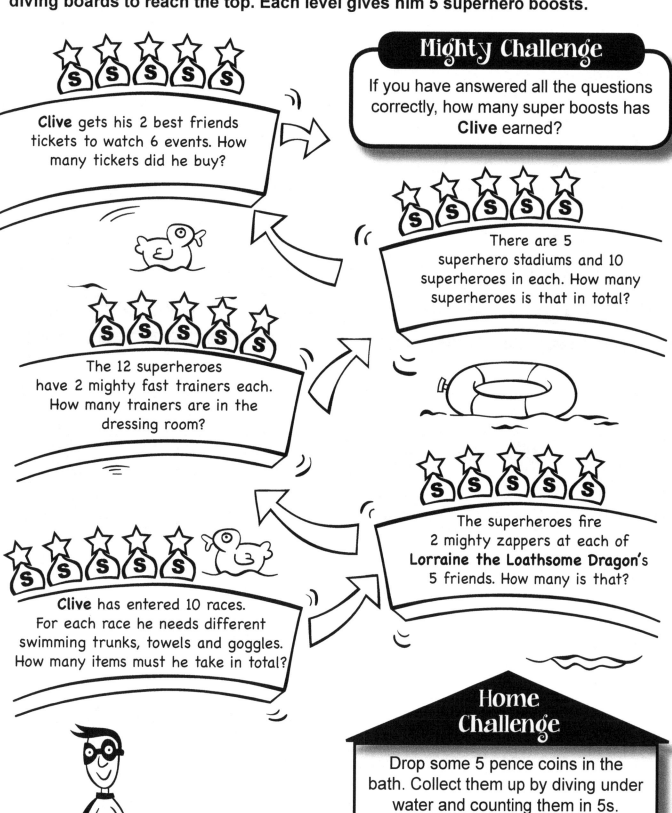

Clive gets his 2 best friends tickets to watch 6 events. How many tickets did he buy?

Mighty Challenge

If you have answered all the questions correctly, how many super boosts has **Clive** earned?

There are 5 superhero stadiums and 10 superheroes in each. How many superheroes is that in total?

The 12 superheroes have 2 mighty fast trainers each. How many trainers are in the dressing room?

The superheroes fire 2 mighty zappers at each of **Lorraine the Loathsome Dragon**'s 5 friends. How many is that?

Clive has entered 10 races. For each race he needs different swimming trunks, towels and goggles. How many items must he take in total?

Home Challenge

Drop some 5 pence coins in the bath. Collect them up by diving under water and counting them in 5s.

Mighty high jumping!

Superheroes must be able to jump mighty high. Match the mighty superheroes to the number sentences on the clouds to help them practise their jumping.

12 x 2

8 x 5

7 x 5

2 x 10

3 x 5

4 x 2

Home Challenge

Can you fly round the room whilst counting is 5s?

Mighty Challenge

Add another cloud and write a question in it that could match one of the superheroes below.

Answers to code sheets

Solve the code   **page 18**
Run mighty fast

Crack the code   **page 23**
In the sandpit

Coded capers   **page 41**
Mighty jumper

Rocket code   **page 50**
Supersonic Sinitta

Lightning Source UK Ltd.
Milton Keynes UK
UKOW07f1330030117

291295UK00001B/13/P